GROUP #11: CONFORMATION INFORMATION

FALL 2002

by Melanie Ann Apel

MAY BE PURCHASED INDIVIDUALLY $13.25
PURCHASE SET & SAVE $$$$

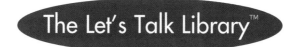

The Let's Talk Library™

Let's Talk About
Being in a Wheelchair

Melanie Ann Apel

The Rosen Publishing Group's

PowerKids Press™
New York

For the Bonnells. Thank you for welcoming me into your family.

Published in 2002 by The Rosen Publishing Group, Inc.
29 East 21st Street, New York, NY 10010

First Edition

Book Design: Colin Dizengoff
Project Editors: Jennifer Landau, Jennifer Quasha, and Jason Moring

Photo Credits: pp. 4, 8 © Photo Researchers; p. 15 © The Image Works; pp. 7, 12, 16, 19 © CORBIS; p. 20 © Medical Library; p. 11 © Archive Photos.

Apel, Melanie Ann.
    Let's talk about being in a wheelchair / Melanie Ann Apel.–1st ed.
         p. cm. — (The let's talk about library)
Includes index.
    ISBN 0-8239-5863-9 (library binding)
    1. Physically handicapped children—Juvenile literature. 2. Handicapped children—Juvenile literature. 3. Wheelchairs—Juvenile literature. [DNLM: 1. Wheelchairs—Juvenile Literature. 2. Disabled Children—Juvenile Literature. WB 320 A641L 2002] I. Title. II.Series.
    RJ47. A635 2002
    617'.03—dc21
                                                                                            00-012038

Manufactured in the United States of America

Contents

Maisy

Maisy does not move around like other kids do. She doesn't run or skip. In fact, even though she is big enough to go to school, Maisy does not even walk. Maisy's legs are not strong. They do not move well. Maisy has an illness that **paralyzed** her legs. Maisy still has to get around, just like everyone else. Maisy has to sit in a special chair when she wants to go places. Maisy's chair has wheels. Maisy's special chair is called a **wheelchair**.

Wheelchairs help people who cannot use their legs to go places.

What Is a Wheelchair?

A wheelchair is a chair on wheels. Anyone who has trouble walking can use a wheelchair to get somewhere. Wheelchairs come in different sizes, just like the people who use them. Some wheelchairs are **motorized**. The person in the wheelchair uses a control to move the chair where he or she wants to go. Some people use their arms to turn the wheels on their wheelchairs. Some people may have trouble moving their arms as well as problems moving their legs. These people need to have their wheelchairs pushed by other people.

Being in a wheelchair can be hard, but with the help of others people still can get places. ▶

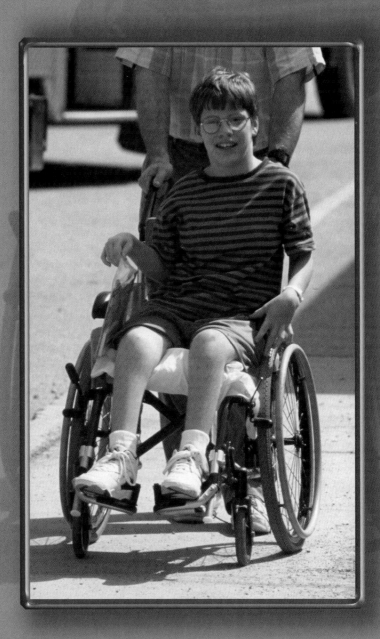

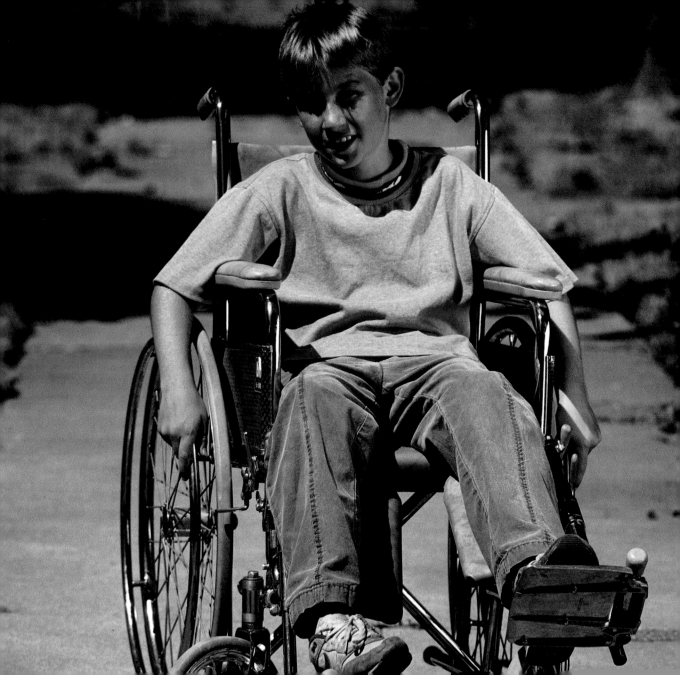

Who Uses a Wheelchair?

Some people use a wheelchair every day. Others use a wheelchair for just a short time. Donna's mom sat in a wheelchair when she brought Donna's baby brother home from the hospital. Tom used a wheelchair until his broken leg was well enough to walk on again. Hayley uses a wheelchair all the time because she was in an accident that paralyzed her legs. Robby's grandpa uses a wheelchair because his legs are too weak to carry him anymore.

People use wheelchairs for many different reasons. Some need them for just a short time. Others need them for longer periods.

Famous People in Wheelchairs

Christopher Reeve is an actor. He played the character Superman in four movies. He had an accident in 1995. He hurt his **spinal cord** very badly. Now he uses a wheelchair to go wherever he wants to go. He makes speeches and does important work from his wheelchair. He was even in a movie in his wheelchair. Another famous person in a wheelchair was Franklin Delano Roosevelt. He was the 32nd president of the United States. His legs became paralyzed from an illness called **polio**.

Christopher Reeve spends much of his time raising awareness about spinal injuries. ▶

Do You Know Someone in a Wheelchair?

Dan's teacher uses a wheelchair. The teenager who takes tickets at the theater uses a wheelchair. Rudy's dad is a doctor who uses a wheelchair. Ariel's aunt is a lawyer who uses a wheelchair. All of these people have regular jobs even though they use wheelchairs. A person in a wheelchair is still a person with thoughts and feelings, just like everyone else. He or she may be very smart. Just because someone's legs do not work well does not mean that the person is really any different from anyone else.

◄ *People who use wheelchairs hold down important jobs, raise families, and do meaningful things in their communities.*

Wheelchair Access

Access means being able to get in and out of places. If you use a wheelchair, you may need special access to a building, a bus, or a sidewalk. Look around your neighborhood. See how the curbs get very low at street corners? That is so a person in a wheelchair can wheel easily across the street without help. Most buildings have ramps outside their doors because people in wheelchairs can't use the stairs. There are special laws to help people in wheelchairs. Wheelchair access lets people who use wheelchairs do the things that everyone else does.

Today there is access to all kinds of places including buildings, homes, cars, and buses. ▶

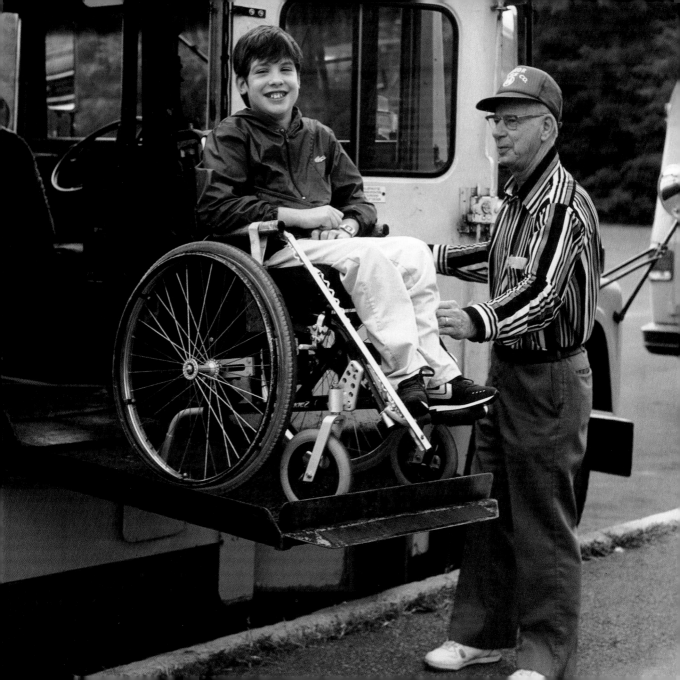

Wheelchair Sports

Kristy's friends play basketball. Kristy joins the game in her wheelchair. Many people in wheelchairs play sports such as softball, basketball, track, tennis, and rugby. There are wheelchair sports organizations and wheelchair events in the **Olympics**. Many people in wheelchairs like to do a sport that does not involve their wheelchairs, such as swimming. A wheelchair doesn't have to stop people from doing things that they enjoy. In fact, it might even take them places they wouldn't have gone without it.

People in wheelchairs have proven to be great athletes, playing all kinds of sports.

Using a Wheelchair for the First Time

Some people who use wheelchairs now did not always use them. Brandon used to walk like other kids. Now he has an illness that makes his legs weak. He had to get used to using a wheelchair. At first he thought it might be fun. When he tried it, it was a little hard to get used to. As Brandon's legs got weaker, he learned to value his wheelchair. Now he is comfortable and goes everywhere in it. When people look at him or ask him about his wheelchair, he tells them, "My legs just don't work very well anymore."

When you first start using a wheelchair, it can be hard to get the hang of it. ▶

Getting in and out of a Wheelchair

Many people in wheelchairs have very strong arms. They use their arms to push the wheelchair. This activity builds muscles. Strong arms also are good for moving into and out of wheelchairs. This is called **transferring**. A man might transfer himself into a wheelchair when he gets out of bed in the morning. A woman might transfer out of her wheelchair when she wants to sit in a regular chair or use the bathroom. If a person needs help transferring, he or she always can ask for help.

◀ *People don't have to spend all their time in a wheelchair. They are able to move themselves in and out of the chairs when necessary.*

Getting Used to a Wheelchair

Using a wheelchair may make a person feel different from other people. Remember that people of all ages use wheelchairs at one time or another, even if only for a short time. Sometimes it takes awhile to get comfortable with a wheelchair. Talking to others who use wheelchairs may make a person feel more comfortable in one. Friends of people in wheelchairs may be curious about wheelchairs and may even want to try them. Letting friends share the experience of using a wheelchair might help you **adapt** to being in a wheelchair regularly.

Glossary

access (AK-sess) A way to get someplace easily.

adapt (uh-DAPT) Change to fit new conditions.

motorized (MOH-tuh-ryzd) Having a motor, which is a machine that produces movement power.

Olympics (uh-LIM-piks) A series of athletic contests for people all over the world, held in different countries every two years.

paralyzed (PAR-uh-lyzd) Unable to feel or move.

polio (POH-lee-oh) A once-common disease that sometimes causes paralysis.

spinal cord (SPY-nal KORD) A thick cord that links the brain to the rest of the nerves in the body.

transferring (TRANS-fer-ing) Moving in and out of a wheelchair.

wheelchair (WEEL-chayr) A chair on wheels used by people who are unable to walk.

Index